GOURMET EXPOSÉ

Revealing Favorite Restaurant Recipes of the Wasatch Front

SUSAN GRIFFIN
JENNIFER AHLSTROM

Illustrated by SONDRA HUDGENS

Dedicated to Dick, Paul, and Clete –
for their support, help, and hearty appetites.

Thanks to friends and family whose encouragement
and continual willingness to sample our creations
made this book possible.

GOURMET EXPOSÉ

It started innocently enough; all we wanted was the recipes from our favorite restaurants. But what started as casual interest became a culinary escapade.

Our amateur sleuthing attempts failed miserably. We tried simple recipe requests, phony concern over food allergies and even considered lab analysis. Then we got serious about our detective work – we kidnapped the chefs and fed them fast food until they talked – and it worked! Then, of course, we had to personally prepare and taste-test Utah's finest restaurant food. For that, our aerobics instructors thank you.

So if you want to savour Utah's best at home, want to entertain, or even want a restaurant tip, we hope you'll enjoy the treasures in this book. Cheers, Utah!

TABLE OF CONTENTS

TABLE OF CONTENTS

TABLE OF CONTENTS

AMERICAN GRILL

Swing into American Grill, a place that puts a modern twist on the hip style of the 1950's. American Grill brings a refined approach to a classic era with a light, cosmopolitan decor and a novel look at American cuisine.

Favorites including hot and cold pasta dishes, grilled meats and fish, and a variety of sandwiches and salads are part of the engaging ensemble. The fantastic dishes are complimented by the lighthearted sounds of your favorite 50's jukebox tunes.

Hop over to either of the two locations for a fun and contemporary dining experience.

1

SPINACH FETTUCCINE

48 oz. spinach fettuccine	1. Cook a la dente.
1/4 cup olive oil (extra virgin) 1/2 cup chicken stock 2 tsp. minced garlic 3 Tbsp. pesto 6 Tbsp. crumbled feta cheese 4 oz. diced prosciutto 1 lb. chicken breasts (diced or julienned) 1/2 cup white wine	2. Add olive oil, chicken stock, minced garlic, and julienned chicken. Saute for 1–2 min. 3. Add remaining ingredients except cream. Simmer for 1 min.
2 cups heavy cream Salt White pepper	4. Add heavy cream, a pinch of salt and white pepper, and let simmer for 2 min. 5. Add cooked spinach fettuccine and bring to a simmer for 1 min. 6. Pour onto serving plate and garnish with asiago or Parmesan cheese.

SERVES 4

FYI:

~ *1 stick of butter can be substituted for the olive oil, if desired.*

TORTILLA SOUP

6 corn tortillas
3 large diced onions
1/8 cup minced garlic
1/2 cup olive oil

1 10 lb. can diced tomatoes
1/2 cup tomato paste
1 gallon chicken stock
1 Tbsp. cumin
1 Tbsp. corriander
3 Tbsp. chili powder
2 bay leaves
1 Tbsp. cayenne
Salt and pepper to taste

1. Saute tortilla strips in olive oil with garlic and onions.

2. Puree diced tomatoes.

3. When onions are translucent and tortillas mushy, add tomatoes. Bring to a boil for 5 minutes.

4. Add remaining ingredients and simmer for 30 minutes.

5. Garnish soup with thinly cut tortilla strips, diced avocado, and grated jack cheese.

SERVES 10–12

FYI:

~ *Tortilla strips used for garnish can be made crispy by deep frying before adding to the soup.*

~ *This recipe makes quite a bit of soup, so freeze the extra for an easy lunch, dinner, or snack.*

ARCHIBALD'S

Take a step back in time and experience the flavor of historic Utah –

delicious country meals and a small town feel (with all of today's amenities).

Archibald's, part of the Gardner Historic Village, is built in a flour mill constructed in 1877. The menu offers cuisine for a variety of appetites – real country cooking with culinary flair. The atmosphere is warm and cozy. It's just right for romantic dinners, family occasions, and perfect for lunch with friends.

The Gardner Village also has some of the best shopping in Utah, especially for country living lovers. Antiques, quilts, homespun wool, and other great treasures can all be found nestled in this quaint village.

And all this in West Jordan, Utah!

SPINACH SALAD
With Hot Bacon Dressing

SPINACH SALAD
1 bunch fresh spinach
3 Tbsp. diced pimentos
2 chopped green onions
1/2 cup sliced mushrooms
1/2 cup shredded monterey jack

2 sliced eggs
1 tomato cut into wedges
1/4 sliced red onion
1/8 cup bacon bits

1. Toss spinach with pimentos, green onions, mushrooms, and cheese.

2. Toss with dressing. Garnish with sliced egg, tomato, red onion slices, and bacon bits.

HOT BACON DRESSING
1/2 lb. bacon
1 cup balsamic vinegar
1 cup water
1/2 lb. brown sugar
2 Tbsp. cornstarch
2 Tbsp. water

1. Brown chopped bacon, do not discard grease.

2. Add balsamic vinegar and water. Bring to a boil. Add brown sugar and return to a boil. Add cornstarch and water until mixture starts to thicken slightly.

SERVES 4

FYI:

~ This makes a large amount of dressing that is best used when fresh.

HALIBUT CASSEROLE
With Tater Chips

2 lbs. fresh halibut
2 cups sliced mushrooms
1 small diced onion
12 oz. shredded cheddar cheese

1. Spray a 13" x 9" casserole dish with cooking spray. Cut boned, skinned halibut into large chunks.

2. Spread halibut in the dish. Sprinkle evenly mushrooms, cheese, and onion with halibut.

16 egg yolks
4 cups heavy cream
Pinch of salt
Pinch of white pepper
2 cups crushed potato chips

3. In mixing bowl, add egg yolks and cream. Add pinch of salt and white pepper and mix well. Pour over halibut mixture.

4. Cover dish with aluminum foil. Bake at 350 degrees for 30 minutes. Remove foil. Bake for additional 15 minutes. Let rest for 20 minutes, top with tater chips and serve.

SERVES 6

FYI:

- You may want to use low cholesterol eggs instead of regular eggs for this recipe.

THE BISTRO ROYALE

Turn off the Main Street of Park City into a comfortable and modern European bistro. The Bistro Royale imports fresh European cuisine, atmosphere and culinary talent into Utah's favorite resort town.

The Master Chef brings the flavor and presentation of a fine European cafe to the alps of Utah. His painstaking attention to detail is demonstrated by the house specialty, the Sleepy Hollow Trout. It's smoked and seasoned in a pan specially designed for the dish.

The Bistro Royale is cozy and chic, however the Chef left two notable items in Europe: cost and calories. The menu is light and healthy, and the only way you can get soaked at this bistro is if you sit too close to the indoor fountain.

SALMON SCALLOPINI

1/4 cup fromage blanch
   or lowfat yogurt
2 1/2 tsp. extra virgin olive oil
1 1/2 tsp. tarragon vinegar
1/4 tsp. Worcestershire sauce
1 1/2 tsp. fresh parsley,
   chopped
1 1/2 tsp. cuervil or dill,
   chopped
1/2 tsp. fresh basil, finely
   chopped
Salt to taste
Fresh ground pepper to taste
1 lb. fillet of salmon, skinned
Sprigs fresh tarragon, dill,
   or cuervil

1. In a small bowl, whisk together fromage blanch or yogurt, 2 Tbsp. warm water, lemon juice, 1 1/2 tsp. oil, vinegar, Worchestershire, herbs, salt and pepper. (This can be prepared up to 10 hours before and chilled)

2. Preheat oven to 500 degrees. Line a baking sheet with aluminum foil, and brush with remaining 1 tsp. oil.

3. Cut salmon in 1/4" thick slices across the grain. Lay scallopinis on the baking sheet and season lightly with salt and pepper.

4. Bake for 1 1/2 to 2 minutes or until fish is opaque.

5. Divide salmon scallopini evenly among 4 plates. Place 1 Tbsp. sauce over each serving. Garnish with sprigs of fresh herbs.

SERVES 4

FYI:

~ *This sauce can also be used as a dip or a salad dressing.*

~ *For the calorie conscious, this is a winner (only 260 calories per serving)!*

PUMPKIN CARAMEL CUSTARD

1 cup sugar
2 cups lowfat milk
1/2 cup cooked pureed
    pumpkin or canned
    pumpkin puree
1/2 cup sugar
4 eggs, lightly beaten
2 Tbsp. vanilla extract
    or one fresh vanilla bean
    cut in half
1 1/2 tsp. ground cinnamon
1/2 tsp. ground nutmeg
1/4 tsp. ground ginger

1. In a heavy-bottomed saucepan, combine sugar and 1/2 cup water. Cook mixture over medium heat, washing down the sides with a brush dipped in water. Once the sugar has dissolved, gently swirl the pan from time to time and cook without stirring until it is a deep orange color.

2. Working quickly, divide the caramel among six 3/4 cup ramequins and swirl the ramequins to coat the bottom and a little on the sides. Preheat oven to 350 degrees.

3. Scald milk in a heavy-bottomed saucepan. In a bowl, combine pumpkin, sugar, egg, vanilla, cinnamon, nutmeg and ginger. Whisk milk into the pumpkin mixture and portion the mixture into the ramequins.

4. Place the ramequins in a baking dish. Cover the tops with a piece of foil and pour hot water into the dish to reach halfway up the outside of the ramequins.

5. Bake for 45-50 minutes or until custards have set. Remove from baking dish and let custards cool on a rack.

6. Run a knife around the sides, invert onto plates and serve warm or chilled.

SERVES 6

FYI:

- The custard can be made up to 2 days ahead and chilled. Before unmolding, place ramequins in a tray with 1/2 inch of hot water and let sit for 5 minutes to melt the caramel.

CAFE PIERPONT

Celebrate good times at Cafe Pierpont, Gastronomy's hot spot for Mexican fare. Located in the renovated Pierpont building that once housed the old Salt Lake High School, Cafe Pierpont features fresh Mexican cuisine, marvelous margaritas, and a cheerful atmosphere.

The fiesta begins as you pass through Cafe Pierpont's revolving doors, entering a scene bursting with color and energy. The eye-catching masks, bright colored ribbons, and outstanding food will make your meal an event to remember.

Specialties at Cafe Pierpont include steaming fajitas, southwestern salads, classic enchiladas, and unusual items such as halibut tacos. Always buzzing with large parties and friends, Cafe Pierpont's lively surroundings make dining a festive event.

POLLO SALAD

POLLO SALAD
12 oz. fresh spinach leaves
1 carrot, shredded
1/2 jicama, shredded
1 cup mandarin orange
   sections
1/2 cup pecan pieces
1/4 cup grated feta cheese
2 6–8 oz. barbecued chicken
   breasts, diced

1. Toss salad ingredients together.

CAESAR SALAD DRESSING
1 1/2 Tbsp. anchovies
2 1/4 tsp. garlic
1 tsp. salt
1 tsp. black pepper
2 Tbsp. Parmesan cheese
2 cups mayonnaise
1 cup red wine vinegar
1 Tbsp. sherry
1 tsp. Worcestershire sauce

1. Mix salad dressing ingredients and toss with above salad.

SERVES 4

FYI:

- Add a dash of lime to the Caesar salad dressing for an added Mexican twist to this delicious salad.

CHICKEN TOSTADA

TOSTADA
2 6–8 oz. boneless chicken breasts
Cajun spice
1/2 avocado, sliced

1/4 head of iceberg lettuce,
    chopped
1 cup romaine lettuce, chopped
3 Tbsp. red onion, chopped
3 tomatoes, chopped
2 Tbsp. feta cheese, grated
2 Tbsp. corn
2 Tbsp. pecan pieces
Tostada shells

1. Dredge chicken in cajun spice and cook in hot skillet or on barbecue until done. Sl chicken. Reserve chicken and sliced avocad

2. Mix remaining ingredients.

3. Top with sliced chicken and sliced avoca

TOMATO/CUMIN DRESSING
1 roasted tomato
2 Tbsp. ground cumin
4 oz. Italian dressing
1 Tbsp. tomato puree

1. Combine all ingredients in a blender unt smooth. Toss with salad ingredients above. Serve on tostada shell.

SERVES 4–6

FYI:

~ The chicken can be served hot or cold. Also, consider using taco bowl shells for serving.

~ The tomato can be roasted by broiling for 5–10 minutes.

CAFE TERIGO

In harmony with the earth, Cafe Terigo provides simple and delicious meals to Park City patrons. The name, Cafe Terigo, reflects its nearness to the land and the bounties provided by our world, Terra Firma.

With a tranquil atmosphere, this cafe offers both deli-style and restaurant items. The store-front features fresh breads, tasty pastries, coffee and desserts, while the restaurant yields light salads, pastas, sandwiches, grilled entrees and innovative daily specials.

Local art and an abundance of fresh flowers enhance your experience at Cafe Terigo as you share in the celebration of our native land.

SPRING PEA SOUP

1/2 cup unsalted butter
1 large yellow onion, chopped
2 Tbsp. flour
1 tsp. curry powder
1/4 tsp. white pepper
1 1/2 tsp. salt
5 cups homemade chicken
  stock
2 lbs. fresh baby peas
  (or frozen petite peas)
1 1/2 tsp. sugar
1 1/2 cups cream

1. Melt butter in large saucepan. Saute onions over medium heat for 5 minutes, or until onion is soft.

2. Add flour and cook for 3 minutes, stirring constantly.

3. Add pepper, salt, curry and chicken stock. Bring to a boil while stirring, scraping the bottom of the pan.

4. Add peas and sugar. Simmer about 4 minutes until the peas are very tender but are still bright green in color. (Be sure not to overcook!)

5. Puree in batches in a blender. Strain to remove skins.

6. Stir in cream. Warm gently, making sure not to bring to a boil. Adjust seasonings to taste.

7. Serve in heated soup bowls. Garnish with croutons or créme fraîche.

SERVES 8

FYI:

~ For a thicker and more textured soup, include the pea skins in the mixture.

SALMON DILL FETTUCCINI

4 Tbsp. unsalted butter
1/4 cup chopped red onion
1/4 cup sliced mushrooms
8 oz. fresh salmon (cut in
   small slices)
4 Tbsp. fresh dill, coarsely
   chopped
2 Tbsp. dry white wine or
   fresh lemon juice
2 cups heavy cream
1/2 tsp. sugar
Salt and pepper to taste
1 lb. fresh spinach fettucini

1. Melt the butter in a medium-sized saute pan over medium heat. Saute onions, mushrooms, and salmon (lightly tossed in flour), for about 2 minutes until the onion is soft.

2. Add wine and deglaze pan. Add dill, saute about 15 seconds.

3. Pour in cream. Season with sugar, salt and pepper. Cook over medium-high heat until the liquid is reduced by almost half. Adjust seasonings.

4. When the sauce is almost reduced, cook the pasta in a large pan of rapidly boiling salted water until al dente, about 3 minutes. Drain in colander.

5. Transfer pasta to large bowl. Pour the salmon sauce over the pasta and toss gently, coating all the pasta. Garnish with lemon and fresh dill sprigs. Serve immediately.

SERVES 4

FYI:

- Fresh dill right out of the garden is a fabulous idea for this recipe!

15

CHARLIE CHOW

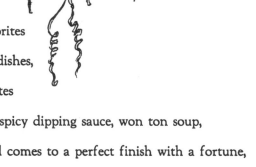

A hot spot for upscale Chinese
cuisine, Charlie Chow is a favorite
with its bright, contemporary design
and acclaimed selection of dishes.

Charlie Chow features Chinese favorites
as well as a wide variety of unique dishes,
all with stylish presentation. Favorites
include Szechuan dumplings with a spicy dipping sauce, won ton soup,
and lemon chicken. And each meal comes to a perfect finish with a fortune,
wrapped ingeniously in a chocolate-covered fortune cookie.

Join in the festivities during Chinese holidays, when Charlie Chow offers
irresistible specials. These original works contain only the freshest ingredients
and are too tempting to miss.

The Trolley Square location makes stopping in for lunch or
dinner convenient and pleasurable for all.

FIRECRACKER NOODLES

FIRECRACKER NOODLES
1/2 lb. fresh Chinese chow
   mein noodles
1/4 tsp. salt
2 Tbsp. soy sauce
1/2 Tbsp. dry sherry
1/2 tsp. sugar
1 Tbsp. Chinese oyster sauce
1 1/2 tsp. sesame oil
1/2 cup chicken stock
1 tsp. fresh minced ginger root
1/4 lb. fresh snow peas
2 green onions
   (cut lengthwise 3")
1/4 cup red bermuda onions
   (cut long)
1 cup Chinese Char Sui Pork
   (see below)

1. Bring water to boil over high heat, add noodles and separate strands. Cook noodles until cooked but firm, about 2–3 minutes. Drain in colander and chill under cold running water. Set aside.

2. When wok is hot enough to sizzle a strand of noodle on contact, shower noodles into wok, toss rapidly. When noodles are at desired crispiness, remove from wok.

3. Add sesame oil and fresh ginger root to wok until ginger is lightly browned. Add snow peas, chicken stock, onions, soy sauce, sherry, sugar, and oyster sauce. Mix well.

4. Add noodles and Char Sui Pork and toss until mixed well.

CHAR SUI PORK
1 lb. lean pork butt
1/2 cup honey
1 tsp. sesame oil

MARINADE
2 Tbsp. dry sherry
1 clove garlic
1 Tbsp. soy sauce
1 tsp. sesame paste
1 tsp. brown bean paste
1 Tbsp. hoisin sauce
1/2 tsp. salt
2 Tbsp. sugar
1/8 tsp. five spice powder

1. Cut pork into 1" x 1" x 8" strips. Combine ingredients for marinade in pan, mix well. Add strips of pork and marinate overnight.

2. Preheat oven to 375 degrees. Fill a roasting pan with water one inch from bottom to prevent drippings from smoking. Place rack on pan, place pork on rack. Brush with honey and oil occasionally, roasting at 450 degrees.

SERVES 6

FYI:

- Pre-cooked Char Sui Pork can be purchased at larger Chinese markets.

POT STICKERS

FILLING
1 1/4 lb. ground pork
1/2 cup scallions, finely cut
1/2 cup chopped nappa cabbage
1 Tbsp. sesame oil
2 tsp. soy sauce
1 1/2 Tbsp. garlic powder
1 egg
1 Tbsp. white wine or
  cooking sherry

1. Mix ingredients well.

POT STICKER SKIN DOUGH
3 cups all-purpose flour
Cold water

1. Add cold water slowly while mixing. Keep adding the cold water and mix until you can form a dough.

2. Take out of bowl and knead until smooth. Sprinkle flour to keep from sticking. When smooth, set aside and cover with a damp cloth until ready to cut into rounds.

3. Cut a portion of dough. Roll and pull into 12" long sausage shape strips. Cut into 12 equal pieces. Roll each piece into a round shape.

4. Fill each skin with a teaspoon of the filling. Fold up into a half moon and pleat one side from one side to the other, keeping one side smooth. Press to seal.

5. Place in boiling water for approximately 3-4 minutes. Remove from water and place on a hot oiled griddle or pan, smooth side down, until golden brown. Serve with soy sauce, rice wine vinegar and hot chili oil.

SERVES 4-6

FYI:

~ For cooks in a hurry, pre-made Gyoza skins can be found in Oriental markets or most grocery stores.

C I S E R O ' S

Cisero's Ristorante and Bar, located at the top of Park City's historic Main Street, is just a step away from the ski slopes and right in the heart of Park City shopping and active nightlife. Cisero's offers two floors of festivities – the Ristorante upstairs and the Bar, a private club for members, downstairs.

The Ristorante upstairs is open for dinner and is a favorite for locals and visitors alike looking for fantastic Italian meals in relaxed, cozy surroundings. For great food and great times, this is the place to be for lunch or dinner.

Find Cisero's Bar, the private club, downstairs and enjoy brunch, lunch, appetizers, and spirits. The regular entertainment – dancing, live music, and a big screen TV – makes it a fun hangout any time of the day.

STUFFED MUSHROOMS

20 large mushroom caps
4 Tbsp. unsalted butter
1/4 cup white wine (chablis)

1. Remove stems and wash. Saute in butter and wine. Cook for 5 minutes and set aside.

1/4 cup diced onions
1/4 cup diced celery
1/4 cup diced red pepper
1 Tbsp. chopped garlic
4 Tbsp. unsalted butter

2. Saute ingredients for 5 minutes then place in mixing bowl and add the following mixture.

1/2 cup bread crumbs
1 cup bay shrimp
2 tsp. parsley flakes
2 tsp. thyme
2 tsp. oregano
2 tsp. basil

3. Mix thoroughly. Adjust consistency with either more bread crumbs or liquid the mushrooms were sauteed in. The shrimp mixture should keep its shape when packed into an ice cream scoop.

4. Place one scoop in each mushroom. Place stuffed mushrooms in an oven-proof dish. Top with Parmesan cheese and bake at 350 degrees for 15–20 minutes.

SERVES 4

FYI:

~ You might try using frozen bay shrimp in the mixture. When the shrimp cool it releases the extra moisture and the result is exceptional, tasty appetizers!

VEAL PICCATA

6 oz. unsalted butter
24 oz. veal, sliced into 2 oz.
    medallions and lightly
    pounded
3 Tbsp. shallots, chopped
Flour

1. Melt butter in large sautee pan. Dredge veal in flour. Cook veal on one side. Add shallots and turn veal over. Do not brown.

1/2 cup white wine
Juice from 2 lemons

2. Add wine and lemon juice and reduce until sauce thickens. Season with salt and pepper.

4 Tbsp. capers
2 oz. unsalted butter

3. Add capers and butter. Once butter melts, serve immediately over your favorite pasta.

SERVES 4

FYI:

- Turkey or pork can be used in place of the veal, if desired.

E . I . B . O . ' S

You'll find yourself in good company at E.I.B.O.'s
It's a popular spot for locals and celebrities alike,
and offers great food in a fun setting.

E.I.B.O.'s is well–known for its unique mesquite broiling.
The mesquite wood (which is trucked in weekly from Mexico)
gives a one–of–a–kind flavor to succulent steaks, mouth–watering ribs,
and other appetizing entrees.

E.I.B.O.'s also highlights a distinguished clientele – the decorated walls feature
signatures and illustrations of celebrities as well as Salt Lake landmarks. Come
hang out at E.I.B.O.'s in Trolley Square and enjoy an upbeat atmosphere,
flavorful meats, and popular names and faces – all at a restaurant that claims
to be "famous for nothing."

WATERMELON BBQ SAUCE

1 stick margarine
1/2 large diced onion
1 diced green pepper

1/2 Tbsp. white pepper
1/2 Tbsp. ground mustard
1 Tbsp. garlic puree
1/2 cup honey
1/4 cup molasses
1/2 tsp. crushed red peppers
1/8 cup dijon mustard
1/2 tsp. watermelon flavoring
2 cups chili sauce
2 cups ketchup
1/2 cup cider vinegar
1/8 cup liquid smoke
1/2 cup brown sugar

1. Saute onions and green peppers in margarine.

2. Add remaining ingredients and simmer for 1 hour.

3. Glaze desired meat and bake, broil, or grill until done.

SERVES 8–10

FYI:

- For exceptional ribs, boil the ribs in water for 1 hour before glazing and broiling or baking.

- You can find watermelon flavoring in specialty bakery stores, and liquid smoke by the BBQ sauce in local grocery stores.

WONTON SALAD

2–3 chicken breasts
1 cup fried wonton strips
1/2 sliced cucumber
1/4 red onion, julienned
5 sliced mushrooms
Cut mixed greens

1. Charbroil chicken and slice into strips.

2. Place fresh mixed greens in salad bowl. Top with cucumber, mushrooms, onions, sliced chicken breast and won tons.

DRESSING
1 cup fresh salsa
1 cup sour cream
1 cup mayonnaise
1/8 cup sesame oil
1/8 cup rice wine vinegar

2. Mix ingredients. Serve salad with dressing on the side.

SERVES 4–6

FYI:

~ *The salad dressing should be fairly thin in consistency. Use fresh salsa to help thin the mixture.*

FERRANTELLI

Experience a walk into Old Italia at Ferrantelli Ristorante
Italiano. Like a relaxed meal in a small sidewalk bistro,
the flavors and personalities of Italy entice you at
Ferrantelli.

The red-checked tablecloths, hanging greenery, and
satisfying Italian cuisine bring East Coast character and influences to Utah.
Enjoy the authentic Northern Italian cuisine with a wide selection of superior
pastas, sauces and specialty dishes.

Italy's unique seasonings and satisfying meals
will warmly greet you at this charming
restaurant in Trolley Square.

MINESTRONE SOUP

1/2 large onion 3 stalks celery 3 medium carrots 1/8 cup garlic puree 1/8 cup butter 1/3 cup flour	1. Saute vegetables in butter and garlic until translucent. Add flour to make roux.
1/2 cup dry white beans 1/2 cup dry red beans 8 cups beef stock 1 Tbsp. basil leaves 1 Tbsp. parsley flakes 1 Tbsp. oregano 1/2 Tbsp. fennel seed 1 Tbsp. thyme leaf 1 lb. pork bones in cheese cloth 6 cups diced tomatoes in juice	2. Soak beans in water for 1 hour. Add beef stock, beans, spices, bones, and tomatoes to vegetable mixture. Cover and simmer for 3 hours.
1/2 lb. diced potatoes	3. Add potatoes and simmer another 1/2 hour.

SERVES 8

FYI:

~ *Simmer on very low heat and cover while you simmer.*

MARINATED VEAL CHOPS

4 veal chops (10–12 oz.)

MARINADE
2/3 cup olive oil
1 Tbsp. minced garlic
1 Tbsp. cracked pepper
2 Tbsp. chopped fresh herbs
   (rosemary, thyme, basil, oregano)
2 Tbsp. lemon juice
2 Tbsp. white wine
4 lemon wedges

1. Place chops in marinade, turning every few hours for at least 12 hours.

2. Broil over hot coals or mesquite wood.

3. Serve with fresh lemon wedges, risotto, and colorful vegetables.

SERVES 4

FYI:

~ Use this wonderful marinade for other meats like chicken or fish.

GIOVANNI'S

Dining in Utah's impressive canyons is an enchanting experience that heightens the senses and soothes the soul. A short drive up Big Cottonwood canyon will bring you to Giovanni's, a hideaway that offers superb Italian specialties with Utah's refreshing appeal.

This cozy restaurant offers excellent cuisine complemented by the spectacular canyon views. The fresh bread and daily soup or salads are an inviting beginning to the meal. And the classic pasta dishes, seafood, and the renown Pepper steak (an absolute must for at least one in your party!) are engaging choices for either a romantic dinner for two or a group celebration.

For a serene and enjoyable evening or relaxed Sunday brunch, visit Giovanni's, and enjoy the mystique and romance of Italian canyon dining.

PEPPER STEAK

4 8oz. fillets of beef
1 cup mango chutney
4 oz. Grand Marnier
4 Tbsp. whole butter
Crushed peppercorns

1. Pound fillets to 1/2 inch thickness.

2. Roll pounded fillets in pepper on one side only.

3. Heat pan until hot, add butter, and melt until butter browns but is not burned.

4. Add fillet, pepper side down on medium–high heat. Sear for 3–5 minutes.

5. Turn and add Grand Marnier and chutney.

6. When steak is done, remove from pan. Finish sauce on low heat, swirling constantly.

7. Pour sauce over steak and serve.

SERVES 4

FYI:

~ Try Major Grey's mango chutney, found in the condiment section at better supermarkets.

GORGONZOLA MUSHROOM SOUP

1/2 onion, chopped
1/2 stalk celery, chopped
1/4 cup shallots, chopped
1/8 cup garlic puree
1 Tbsp. whole butter
1/2 lb. Porcini mushrooms
1 gallon chicken stock
1 quart heavy cream
1 cup crumbled Gorgonzola
  cheese
1/4 cup chicken base
White pepper to taste
Salt to taste

1. Saute onions, celery, shallots and garlic in whole butter until transluscent.

2. Add mushrooms and chicken stock. Simmer for 20 minutes.

3. Add cream, Gorgonzola cheese, chicken base, and salt and pepper. Simmer for 10 minutes.

4. Puree mixture. For thicker soup, let boil and reduce. For garnish, cut additional Porcini mushrooms in half, saute in butter, and add to soup.

SERVES 8

FYI:

~ *Porcini mushrooms and Gorgonzola cheese can be found at Granato's Italian Foods, along with many other Italian goodies.*

HIBACHI

Located in the heart of Salt Lake City is Hibachi, a quaint Japanese restaurant that serves some of the finest Japanese cuisine available. Hibachi provides lunch and dinner items in two distinct atmospheres, both with outstanding service and exceptional meals.

Hibachi is an ideal location for a casual lunch. In fact, our regular visits to Hibachi (we come for the salad dressing alone!) inspired the creation of this cookbook. Entrees are served over rice, or with Donburi, thick noodles in a tasty broth.

Dinner at Hibachi is a more traditional Japanese dining experience. Enjoy the solitude of a private room while you dine on tempura, teriyaki, or an assortment of dishes with Hibachi's outstanding spicy sauce. And because Japanese customs prevail during your meal, shoes are taboo!

CHICKEN TERIYAKI

4 chicken breasts

1. Prepare frying pan with oil. Fry chicken until done. Cut into 1/2" strips.

TERIYAKI SAUCE
1/3 cup Kikkoman soy sauce
2 slices fresh ginger
5 Tbsp. sugar
5 tsp. Japanese rice vinegar
1 2/3 cups water
3 tsp. cornstarch

2. Mix soy sauce, ginger, sugar, rice vinegar and water. Bring mixture to a boil. Reduce heat and allow to simmer for 4–5 minutes. Remove ginger slices. Add cornstarch mixed with water to thicken.

3. Pour sauce over chicken and serve with a side of Oriental rice. Sprinkle with sesame seeds. Garnish with pickled lettuce and carrots.

SERVES 4

FYI:

~ You can sweeten this sauce by adding more sugar, or if a saltier version is preferred, reduce the amount of water.

J A P A N E S E   S A L A D

Lettuce of choice
Assorted vegetables

1. Tear lettuce of choice. Chop assorted vegetables and toss with salad.

SALAD DRESSING
1 cup mayonnaise
1/2 tsp. white pepper
1/4–1/2 tsp. sesame oil
2 Tbsp. lemon juice
1/3 cup sugar
5 Tbsp. milk

2. Mix together mayonnaise, white pepper, sesame oil, lemon juice, and sugar.

3. When ready to serve, add milk and mix well.

SERVES 4

FYI:

~ Like we said, this incredible salad dressing was the inspiration for this book. It is one of our all-time favorites!

HUNGRY I

Discover rare treasures of the Mediterranean at Hungry I.
Greek and Northern Italian specialties are featured here
in a light, cosmopolitan setting. Hungry I offers extraordinary
lunch, dinner and Sunday brunch items, and is an ideal
location for special occasions or romantic dinners.

The food is masterful, with traditional Greek and Northern
Italian dishes served aside fresh and new creations.
Favorites include the ribs with homemade dijon–anise
barbeque sauce, Utah lamb, and the famous Avgolemeno
soup. Memorable additions to the meal include the fresh
french bread served with a dipping sauce of extra virgin
olive oil, garlic and balsamic vinegar, and the savory
desserts, all made on the premises with authentic recipes.

For a unique taste of Salt Lake, visit Hungry I
and enjoy a cultural and palatable Grecian
experience.

AVGOLEMENO SOUP

One small, whole chicken
3 quarts chicken broth
3/4 cup Orzo noodles or
   long grain rice
Salt to taste
White pepper to taste
5 beaten eggs
3/4 cup lemon juice
1 1/2 Tbsp. flour

1. In large stock pot, combine chicken stock and whole chicken. Bring to boil. Simmer until chicken is fully cooked.

2. Remove chicken and pull off all meat, discarding bones and skin. Cut chicken into 1/4 inch pieces, reserve in separate container.

3. Bring broth to boil, add Orzo or rice and simmer approximately 20 minutes or until tender.

4. In a large mixing bowl, combine eggs, lemon juice, and flour. Beat thoroughly.

5. Skim 2 cups of hot broth from the stock pot and slowly beat into the egg mixture. Slowly add the egg and broth mixture to the stock pot while stirring constantly.

6. Cook over low heat for about 7 minutes. (Do not allow soup to boil or it will curdle.)

7. Add diced chicken, salt and pepper, and serve.

SERVES 8–10

FYI:

~ *This ancient Greek chicken noodle soup is a daily favorite at the Hungry I.*

PSARI PLAKI

Olive oil
2 cloves garlic, chopped
1 stalk celery, chopped
1/2 large onion, chopped

1. Preheat oven to 350 degrees. Heat 2 Tbsp. olive oil in skillet. Add garlic, celery, and onion. Saute until celery and onion are almost translucent. Remove from heat.

2 1/2 lbs. fresh fish fillets
  (snapper, halibut, or other)
Olive oil
3-4 diced tomatoes
3 Tbsp. fresh dill
  (finely chopped)
Salt to taste
Fresh ground black pepper
1/4 cup dry white wine
10 Greek olives
1/2 cup feta cheese, grated

2. In baking dish, add approximately 2 Tbsp. olive oil and place fish in pan. Mix tomato and dill. Top fish with onion mixture, salt and pepper, and tomato mixture.

3. Pour wine over fish and add olives. Bake for approximately 20 minutes or until tender.

4. Sprinkle top with grated feta cheese and bake for an additional 5 minutes. If necessary, add water to keep moist while baking.

SERVES 4

FYI:

~ *The fish may take less than 20 minutes to bake, so be careful not to overcook.*

~ *Additional feta cheese can be added to taste.*

LA CAILLE

A place of wonder and elegance, La Caille at Quail Run
offers exquisite food in a charming setting. Within minutes of Salt
Lake, you will find a hidden treasure of gardens, wildlife, and fine
dining.

Dining in the traditional French chateau offers authentic French
country cuisine. Sunday brunch, dinners, and Basque dinners are
prepared with great care. Utah's seasons come alive at La Caille
and present fresh spring flowers, outdoor evening dining, bursts of
fall colors, and winter warmth and electricity.

Antiques are abundant in the spacious chateau and are French country
originals. The many rooms of the chateau are ideal for intimate
dinners or group gatherings.

So forget about your daily worries and responsibilities
and retreat to a place of beauty in rural France.
Your experience at La Caille will surely be
a memorable one.

S A L M O N   R O L L S

PUFF PASTRY
1 3/4 cups flour
1 oz. lard
6 oz. puff paste
2 Tbsp. lemon juice
4 to 4 1/2 oz. water

1. Rub flour and lard together, add liquids. Knead dough for 10 min. or put under dough hook 6–7 min. This dough must be well developed. Turn onto floured surface and let rest 10 min.

2. Roll in rectangle about 12" x 8". Cover 2/3 of dough with roll–in compound. Fold uncovered side over, then other side over so that you have dough/fat/dough/fat. Let rest 10 min. between each turn. Place in refrigerator overnight.

3. Remove from refrigerator and let the puff dough become warm in the kitchen about an hour before use. Roll out to about 1/8" thickness.

SALMON MIXTURE
1 lb. salmon meat
1/4 cup chopped celery
1/4 cooked onion
1/4 cup cooked white rice
1/4 to 1/2 cup mayonnaise
Salt and pepper to taste

4. Cook salmon in 2 cups water with onion and celery. Remove salmon, reduce the stock by half, reserve for glaze. Mix all ingredients and spoon or pipe into pastry.

5. Fold dough around mixture and seal with egg wash. Bake 45–60 min. at 425 degrees.

GLAZE
2 cups salmon stock
1/2 cup dry sherry
4 Tbsp. tomato puree
4 slices green pepper
2 pinches each ham and
   chicken bullion

6. Put on high heat and bring all ingredients to a boil for 10–15 min. Spoon over salmon roll before serving.

SERVES 4

FYI:

~ *You can buy puff pastry at the grocery store if you don't have the time (or the patience) to make the puff paste.*

BLACK TIGER PRAWNS (Thai Style)

3/4 cup dark soy sauce
3/4 cup water
6 tsp. balsamic vinegar
2 Tbsp. fresh minced ginger
6 Tbsp. sugar

1. Bring soy sauce, water, vinegar, and ginger to a boil. Add sugar and simmer for 15 minutes.

8 pcs. shitake mushrooms
1/2 red pepper
1/2 green pepper
2 Tbsp. spring onion
   (finely chopped)
2 small red chili peppers
   (seeded and chopped)

2. Julienne mushrooms, red and green pepper. Add mushrooms, bell peppers, onion and chili. Cook until vegetables are tender.

1/4 cup water
2 Tbsp. cornstarch

3. Mix the cornstarch with 1/4 cup water to thin paste. Slowly stir into sauce and simmer for 5 minutes. Reserve, keep warm.

20 pcs. tiger prawns
   (peeled, cleaned, deveined)
4 scoops white sticky rice
20 pcs. snow peas, blanched
1 sprig fresh watercress
Pickled ginger

4. Season prawns with salt and pepper. Heat a saute pan with clarified butter, add prawns and saute until just firm.

5. Meanwhile, place rice in the center of the plate, then place 5 prawns around the rice and spoon sauce over the prawns. Top with pickled ginger. Place 5 snow pea pods in between each prawn and garnish with watercress.

SERVES 4

FYI:

~ The is an easy, but impressive dish, so you may want to double it if you have a bigger crowd.

LAMB'S

Ahh, landmarks. In the heart of downtown Salt Lake City lies Lamb's Restaurant, the oldest restaurant in Utah. Lamb's features classic cooking (where else can you find a perfect rendition of liver and onions?) in a relaxed and historic atmosphere.

Lamb's is famous for (you guessed it) lamb, but it also features satisfying lunch and dinner choices such as fresh seafood, steaks, or chops, all served with soup, bread, salad and dessert. Breakfast is a hot item at Lamb's, and regulars can be found in their favorite spot at the marble-topped counter for coffee and eggs. Lunch and dinner specials, served at the counter or in the large dining areas, are enjoyed by the business-minded as well as tourists, shoppers and theater-goers.

Lamb's enduring success is due to its consistently good food, exceptional service and reasonable prices. Eating at Lamb's is a delightful experience – a Utah showcase at its oldest and best!

BARBECUED LAMB SHANKS

6 lamb shanks (12 oz. each)
2 Tbsp. paprika
1 Tbsp. garlic powder
1 tsp. allspice
Salt to taste
Fresh ground black pepper
2 medium onions, chopped
3–4 cups beef stock
1 can (8 oz.) tomato sauce
1 can (6 oz.) tomato paste
2 Tbsp. lemon juice
Chopped fresh parsley

1. Wash lamb shanks; place in large pot or roasting pan. Combine paprika, garlic powder, and allspice. Rub into meat. Add salt and pepper as desired. Sprinkle with chopped onions. Cover and refrigerate overnight.

2. Preheat oven to 375 degrees. Bake lamb shanks without adding liquid for about two hours, turning occasionally until brown. When brown, add about 1 cup beef stock. Bake about 30 minutes.

3. Remove from oven. Place on stove over medium heat. Cover shanks with beef stock. Remove lamb shanks from pot. Skim fat from broth. Add tomato sauce, tomato paste and lemon juice; stir to blend. Season sauce with salt, pepper, and garlic powder as desired.

4. Return shanks to pan. Simmer over low to medium heat for about two hours or until meat is tender. Sauce should not be too thin. If necessary, thin with more beef stock or thicken with a little flour whipped in cold water.

5. Place shanks on heated serving platter. Top with sauce, then sprinkle with chopped parsley.

SERVES 6

FYI:

~ We suggest that you serve this distinctive dish with rice pilaf, Greek salad, fresh bread, and Lamb's Rice Pudding (also included in this book). It's an impressive meal for dinner guests!

RICE PUDDING

1 cup long grain rice
1 cup sugar
8 cups milk
4 eggs
2 cups milk
1/4 cup sugar
2 tsp. vanilla
Ground cinnamon

1. In large saucepan, combine rice with 1 cup sugar and 8 cups milk. Stir to blend. Cook, covered, until rice is tender.

2. In mixing bowl, combine eggs and 2 cups milk with 1/4 cups sugar and vanilla. Beat well.

3. When rice is tender, add egg mixture. Cook until mixture just starts to boil, stirring occasionally. Remove from heat. Cool then chill.

4. Serve topped with a sprinkle of ground cinnamon.

SERVES 6–8

FYI:

~ This versatile dish can be used as an elegant dessert or an afternoon snack for the family.

MANDARIN

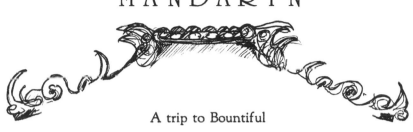

A trip to Bountiful

will bring you to a land of plenty. The Mandarin Restaurant, located

just 10 minutes north of Salt Lake, provides a unique and upscale setting for

its 190 seat Chinese restaurant.

This thriving restaurant offers spectacular Oriental food that is fresh, crisp, and

flavorful. Almond chicken, beef with asparagus, and Szechuan shrimp

are a few of the popular choices on the menu. The

Mandarin also offers an assortment of appetizers,

Oriental salads, fresh seafood specials, intriguing

desserts, and imported teas and beverages.

As a family-run business, the Mandarin excels in efficient

and knowledgeable service. In fact, the only thing that's

scarce at the Mandarin is an empty table

on a weekend night!

BEEF & ASPARAGUS
With Black Bean Sauce

6 oz. flank steak
10 oz. fresh asparagus
8 oz. vegetable oil

1. Cut steak into 3" x 2" x 1/8" slices. Add the oil to a hot wok. When oil is very hot, stir–fry the asparagus for 5 seconds. Strain the asparagus and leave oil in wok.

2. Stir–fry the flank steak for 15 seconds. Strain the flank steak from the oil and save the oil for future stir–fry.

1 Tbsp. vegetable oil
1 Tbsp. fermented black beans
1 tsp. (heaping) minced garlic
6 oz. low sodium chicken broth
1 tsp. dark soy sauce
1 tsp. oyster sauce
1 tsp. hoisin sauce
1 Tbsp. sherry wine
1/4 tsp. salt
1/2 tsp. sugar
Dash of white pepper

3. To a hot wok, add the vegetable oil, garlic, and black beans. Saute for 3 seconds. Add the flank steak and asparagus and stir–fry for 3 seconds.

4. Add the chicken broth and remaining ingredients. Stir–fry for 10 seconds.

1 tsp. cornstarch
2 tsp. chicken broth
1/2 tsp. sesame oil

5. Dissolve the cornstarch in the chicken broth and add to the wok. Stir–fry till the sauce thickens. Add sesame oil and stir–fry for 2 seconds.

SERVES 4

FYI:

~ *Serve this wonderful dish with Oriental rice and complementary dishes such as Phoenix and Dragon (on following page).*

PHOENIX & DRAGON

3 1/2 oz. chicken breast
3 1/2 oz. peeled shrimp
(size 31–40)
8 oz. vegetable oil

1. Cut the chicken in 1" x 1" x 1/2" strips. Add the oil to a hot wok. When oil is very hot, add the chicken and shrimp and stir-fry for 15 seconds. Strain the shrimp and chicken from the oil and save the oil for future stir-fry.

1/4 cup waterchestnuts,
sliced
1/4 cup bamboo shoots,
sliced
6 pieces red bell pepper,
cut into 1" squares
10 pieces carrot,
1" x 2" x 1/8"
12 pieces snow pea
6 pieces napa, cut into
1" squares
6 pieces baby corn
12 pieces straw mushroom
6 pieces broccoli flowerettes

2. Blanch the vegetables in very hot water for 1 minute, then strain.

1 tsp. vegetable oil
1 tsp. (heaping) minced garlic
1 tsp. minced ginger
5 oz. low sodium chicken broth
1 Tbsp. sherry wine
1/2 tsp. salt
1 tsp. oyster sauce
1/2 tsp. sugar
Dash white pepper

3. To a very hot wok, add the vegetable oil, garlic and ginger. Stir-fry for 3 seconds. Add the chicken, shrimp, vegetables, chicken broth and remaining ingredients and stir-fry for 10 seconds.

1 tsp. cornstarch
2 tsp. chicken broth
1/2 tsp. sesame oil

4. Dissolve cornstarch in the chicken broth and add to the wok. Stir-fry until sauce thickens. Add sesame oil and stir-fry for 2 seconds.

SERVES 4

MARKET STREET BROILER

It's so fresh, it should be slapped.
F-R-E-S-H is the word for Market Street Broiler's
menu selection — featuring exceptional
fish and seafood specials. The fish, flown
in daily from both coasts, is prepared in
countless ways (the mesquite grill being
a particular favorite). As the grill heats up
the glassed-in kitchen provides an open view
to diners awaiting their catch of the day, ribs, or other
savory selections.

Located near the University of Utah in what used to be
Fire Station No. 8, the Market Street Broiler sounds the alarm
for great restaurant dining as well as convenient take-home
items. The fresh fish, pastries, breads, salads, and famous
clam chowder are unforgettable additions to any meal.

So whether it's grilled, baked, sauteed, fried,
or blackened, the Market Street Broiler will
serve it to perfection, and that's no fish tale!

APPLE PIE

PIE FILLING
7 golden delicious apples,
   pared, cored and sliced
2 Tbsp. lemon juice
1 1/2 cups sugar
1 tsp. cinnamon
1/4 tsp. nutmeg
1/4 tsp. allspice
3 rounded Tbsp. cornstarch
Pinch salt
1/2 cup water
3 Tbsp. butter

1. Toss apples with lemon juice. In a sauce pan, combine sugar, cinnamon, nutmeg, allspice, salt and cornstarch. Mix well. Add water and butter, mixing well.

2. Place over heat and bring to a boil, stirring occasionally. Remove from heat and toss with sliced apples. Turn into bottom crust. Place top crust, adding steam vents. Seal and crimp.

3. Bake 15 minutes at 375 degrees, then an additional 45 minutes at 350 degrees.

PIE CRUST
2 cups flour
1 tsp. sugar
1 tsp. salt
1 tsp. baking powder
1/2 cup butter
1/2 cup shortening
1/2 cup cold water

1. Stir together flour, sugar, salt and baking powder. Add butter and shortening. Cut into flour mix with fork or pastry blender until mixture resembles crumbs.

2. Add, all at once, cold water. Stir by hand with a fork until incorporated and can be handled.

3. When ready to use, divide dough in half. Roll out each half on floured board to fit bottom and top of 10 inch pie plate. Reserve top crust to add after filling is placed in crust. Makes one double crust pie or two pie shells.

SERVES 6–8

FYI:

~ This recipe is an outstanding version of an American classic!

CRAB CAKES

1 heaping Tbsp. chopped
  green pepper
1 heaping Tbsp. chopped
  red onion
1/4 cup tartar sauce
1 egg
1 tsp. Old Bay seasoning
1/2 cup bread crumbs
1 lb. Canadian snow crab

1. Mix ingredients and chill for at least 20 minutes.

2. Form crab cakes into patties.

3. Fry cakes in a small amount of oil. Garnish with lemon wedges and a side of tartar sauce.

TARTAR SAUCE
1 cup mayonnaise
2 Tbsp. minced dill pickle
  or dill relish
2 Tbsp. minced onion
1 Tbsp. chopped parsley
1 Tbsp. chopped capers
2 Tbsp. caper juice
Juice of 1/2 medium lemon
1/4 tsp. white pepper
1/4 tsp. salt
1 oz. buttermilk

1. Combine all ingredients and refrigerate 30 minutes.

SERVES 4

FYI:

~ *As a meal, this serves 2 and as an appetizer, it serves 4.*

~ *Additional tartar sauce can be used in the mixture if the cakes are too dry.*

McHENRY'S GRILL

If you're planning a visit to Deer Valley, make McHenry's Grill part of your itinerary. McHenry's Grill is located in Deer Valley's Silver Lake Lodge just minutes from Main Street. Ski, bike, hike, or enjoy a leisurely chairlift ride to the top of Bald Mountain. Then, come experience the casual atmosphere with scenic deck dining and a menu the entire family can enjoy.

The menu includes creative appetizers, salads, gourmet pizzas, specialty sandwiches and the famous Deer Valley Burger. Bike shorts, business suits and ski boots are all welcome, so come as you are to McHenry's Grill.

McHenry's Grill is open for the winter and summer months.

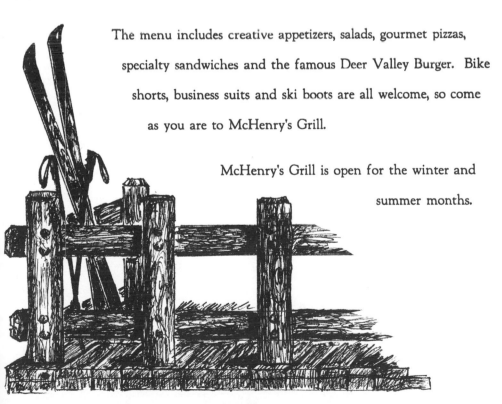

SUN-DRIED TOMATO & PESTO MASCARPONE TERRINE

MASCARPONE
1 1/2 lbs. cream cheese,
    softened
1 lb. whole butter, softened
2 tsp. black pepper
1/2 tsp. salt

1. Puree in processor until smooth. Reserve at room temperature.

PESTO
2 cups fresh basil, tightly packed
1/2 cup pine nuts, toasted
1/2 cup grated Parmesan cheese
1/4 cup minced garlic
1/2 cup olive oil
1 tsp. salt
2 tsp. black pepper

2. Puree in processor until smooth but still particulate. Reserve at room temperature.

DRIED TOMATO PUREE
2 cups drained sun-dried
    tomatoes
1 Tbsp. chopped marjoram
2 tsp. minced garlic
1 tsp. black pepper

3. Blend tomatoes and other ingredients in processor until smooth. Reserve at room temperature.

SERVES 10–12

4. Line a 4–6 cup serving bowl (or mixing bowl) with plastic wrap so about 2" hangs over the rim. Make the wrap as wrinkle free as possible on the inside of the bowl. Begin filling the bowl with alternating layers of ingredients as follows:
    1/2" cheese, 1/4" pesto, 1/2" cheese, 1/4" tomato puree, etc.

5. Make each layer a uniform thickness. After adding a layer, tap base of bowl on table to eliminate air pockets. When final layer is added (cheese layer should be last), cover with plastic and refrigerate 4 hours.

6. To serve, remove cover of plastic wrap and invert onto serving platter making sure the excess plastic lining is not underneath the mold. If the terrine does not unmold by itself, pull the edges of the plastic liner to help remove it from the bow Once unmolded, remove plastic wrap. Arrange your favorite crackers, toasts or breads around the terrine.

FROZEN LEMON MERINGUE PIE

CRUST
1 1/2 cups graham
   cracker crumbs
1/4 cup sugar
1/4 cup melted butter

1. Combine ingredients. Press into 10" pie tin. Pre-bake five minutes to set.

FILLING
Zest of two lemons
1 cup fresh lemon juice
26 oz. sweetened,
   condensed milk
8 oz. cream cheese
8 egg yolks

2. In food processor, puree yolks, add half of lemon juice, add half of milk, then the cream cheese. Scrape well.

3. Add remaining milk, then juice and zest. Pour into prepared crust and freeze.

TOPPING
1 cup egg whites
Pinch of cream of tartar
1 cup and 2 Tbsp. sugar

4. In clean bowl, whisk egg whites with cream of tartar until soft peaks form. Gradually sprinkle in sugar and beat until very stiff.

5. Spread 1 cup meringue on frozen lemon filling. With large star tip in a pastry bag, pipe remaining meringue in rosettes to mark each piece.

6. Bake for five minutes in pre-heated 500 degree oven to brown meringue. Serve frozen, but tempered.

SERVES 8-10

FYI:

~ For outstanding meringue, add sugar to mixture VERY slowly and do not overbeat.

MIKADO

Get away to the Far East this weekend.
For thirty-five years, the Mikado has been Salt Lake
City's portal to Old Japan.

As the kimono-clad waitress escorts you to the privacy
of your own Zashiki room, it's easy to forget that you
are in Salt Lake City. The Mikado's simple lines, delicate
paper walls, and elegant decorations create a tranquil
dining atmosphere.

The Mikado serves a wide variety of seafood and
traditional Japanese dishes. Beef Sukiyaki, Bata Yaki,
and Shabu Shabu can all be prepared at your table by
talented and entertaining chefs.

You don't need to go to Japan to get away – the Mikado
is your passport to fine Japanese dining.

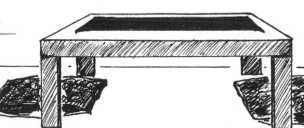

MOUNTAIN TROUT

2 cups onion, chopped
3 cups mushrooms, sliced
4 black tiger jumbo shrimp, chopped
4–8 scallops, chopped
6 Tbsp. oyster sauce
2 tsp. fresh grated ginger
1 cup teriyaki sauce
4 fresh trout, butterflied

1. Saute onions in butter. Add mushrooms. Add shrimp, scallops, oyster sauce, ginger, and teriyaki sauce (in that order).

2. Reduce to desired consistency.

3. Broil or grill butterflied trout until done. Pour sauce over trout. Garnish with sliced almonds and lemon wedges.

SERVES 4

FYI:

~ *This makes an ample amount of sauce that could be used for additional pieces of trout.*

B E E F   S U K I Y A K I

SUKIYAKI SAUCE
1 cup soy sauce
3/4 cup sugar
5 cups water

1. Bring ingredients to a slow boil for 15 minutes.

BEEF SUKIYAKI
1/2 bunch green onions
1/2 cup bamboo shoots
2-4 inch cube of tofu
1 cup sliced mushrooms
1/2 cup chopped onion
6 cups chopped napa cabbage
10 oz. thinly sliced ribeye steak
3 cups saifun noodles

2. Simmer vegetables in sukiyaki sauce until tender. Add beef and cook until desired doneness.

3. Cook saifun noodles according to package directions. Add noodles to Sukiyaki and serve.

SERVES 4

FYI:

- We suggest that you serve the Sukiyaki with other traditional Japanese dishes, such as tempura or sushi.

MILETI'S

If you don't have a "favorite little Italian place", you

haven't been to Mileti's. Located on Main Street in Park City,

Mileti's has become synonymous with great Italian food and lively Park

City nightlife since 1973.

Mileti's ecclectic lavender and green decor, and wood tables with pewter accents

provide a fun, non-traditional setting for truly distinctive Italian food. It's hard

to say the words Pesto Lasagna, Capellini Tuttomare, or Scampi Mediterranean

without activating your tastebuds.

Whether you're socializing in Mileti's private club upstairs, or enjoying fine Italian

dining downstairs, Mileti's endearing qualities will bring you back again and again.

PESTO LASAGNA

PESTO
1 cup lightly packed fresh
  basil leaves, washed and dried
1/4 cup grated Parmesan
1/4 cup olive oil

1. Place basil and Parmesan in food processor. Add oil in slow stream until basil is finely chopped.

LASAGNA
2 eggs
2 cups ricotta cheese
2 cups cottage cheese
1 cup Parmesan cheese
1 lb. lasagna noodles
1 1/2 cups Italian tomato
  sauce
1 1/2 cups tomatoes, diced
1 cup spinach, diced
1/4 cup red onion, diced
Salt and pepper to taste

2. For cheese mixture, beat eggs in mixing bowl. Add ricotta and cottage cheeses and 1/2 cup Parmesan cheese. Whisk until smooth.

2. Cook lasagna noodles in boiling water until al dente. Lightly oil a 9" x 13" baking dish.

3. Coat bottom with 3/4 cup Italian tomato sauce. Place an even layer of noodles on sauce. Add 1/2 of cheese mixture.

4. Smear pesto evenly on next layer of noodles and then place noodles on cheese layer.

5. Top with diced tomatoes, spinach and red onions. Lightly salt and pepper diced tomatoes.

6. Add the third layer of noodles. Spoon on rest of the cheese mixture. Add final layer of noodles. Top with rest of tomato sauce and sprinkle with 1/2 cup Parmesan.

7. Bake uncovered in a 300 degree oven for 60 minutes or until top is crusty and sauce is bubbly. Cut into squares to serve.

SERVES 6–8

FYI:

~ *If you don't have time to make your own pesto, you can buy it pre-made from most grocery stores.*

TEXAS BBQ SHRIMP

4 skewers
16 jumbo shrimp,
   peeled and deveined
16 thin slices jalapeno,
   approximately 1" long
8 strips thin sliced, hickory
   smoked bacon
1 cup barbeque sauce
4 lemon wedges

1. Cut bacon strips in half. Place jalapeno strip along back of shrimp where deveined.

2. Wrap bacon tightly around shrimp and jalapeno, being careful to not overlap bacon too much.

3. Slide four of the shrimp onto each skewer, so they lay flat upon grill. Cook over charcoal until bacon is brown and shrimp are done.

4. Baste with barbecue sauce and serve with lemon wedge.

SERVES 4

FYI:

- This is a wonderful appetizer for outdoor cooking – an it's not too hot, even with jalapenos!

MILLCREEK INN

A leisurely drive up Millcreek Canyon will bring you to Millcreek Inn – a restaurant tailored for quiet evenings away from the hustle of the city. Set amidst the stream and pines, it's perfect for a romantic dinner for two as well as a charming reception.

As the seasons change, so does the atmosphere at Millcreek Inn. Savor exquisite cuisine by the warmth of the fire as snow falls softly outside, or enjoy dining on the patio where breezes cool down the hot summer nights.

Retreat to Millcreek Inn and relish an afternoon or evening of refined dining in an unspoiled setting.

M I L L C R E E K   D U C K

1 duck
Fresh rosemary to taste
Fresh thyme to taste
Granulated garlic to taste
Salt
Pepper

1. Remove gizzards from duck. Stuff with rosemary and thyme. Top with salt, pepper, and garlic.

2. Bake at 400 degrees for two hours or until done.

3. After baking in oven, cut duck in half. Remove all bones except the main wing bone and thigh bone.

1/2 cup chicken stock
1/8 cup brandy
1/4 cup triple sec
1/2 cup strawberries
1 1/4 cup brown sauce

4. Place duck in saute pan with chicken stock, triple sec, brandy, and strawberries. Simmer for 10 minutes.

5. Remove duck and place in oven until crispy. Add brown sauce to strawberry mixture and continue simmering until desired consistency.

6. Place sauce over duck and serve.

SERVES 2

FYI:

~ For brown sauce, you can try Knorr's Demi–Glace in a dry mix package. It's a tasty brown sauce and is effortless to make!

~ The serving size of this dish depends on the size of your duck. For presentation purposes, it's more attractive if this is a 2 person serving.

CHICKEN LORRAINE

STUFFING
1/2 cup chopped spinach
1 1/2 cups sliced mushrooms
1 Tbsp. butter
2 Tbsp. sherry
1 Tbsp. chopped shallots
Salt to taste
Pepper to taste
2 Tbsp. chicken stock
1/4 cup cream
1 Tbsp. flour

1. Cook spinach and mushrooms in butter, sherry, shallots, salt, pepper, and chicken stock until spinach is cooked. Add cream and flour to thicken. Let cool.

4 split chicken breasts
Feta cheese to taste
Flour
Bread crumbs
Eggs
Vegetable oil

2. Stuff chicken breasts with spinach mixture and feta cheese. Partially freeze for ease of future handling.

3. Set up breading station with flour, egg wash, and bread crumbs. Flour chicken breasts, dip in egg wash, and roll in bread crumbs.

4. Deep fry in 350 degree oil until golden brown. Bake in oven at 350 degrees for 20–30 minutes or until done.

SAUCE
1/4 cup maderia wine
1 Tbsp. shallots
1/4 cup chicken stock
1 Tbsp. basil
1/2 cup brown sauce

5. Flame the maderia wine. Add remaining ingredients and simmer until desired consistency. Pour over chicken and serve.

SERVES 4

FYI:

~ Try using toothpicks to hold the chicken together during frying and baking.

~ For brown sauce, you can try Knorr's Demi-Glace in a dry mix package. It's a tasty brown sauce and is effortless to make!

THE NEW YORKER

The New Yorker sets the stage for fashionable dining in Salt Lake City. Located in the aptly named New York Building, the New Yorker receives high marks for its continental cuisine and distinguished atmosphere.

The dining room and Cafe at the New Yorker present daily performances of superb entrees and exquisite desserts that receive rave reviews from downtown visitors. With banquet rooms that can accommodate groups of 4 to 40, the upscale setting invites both a casual and fine dining crowd.

Critics agree that the New Yorker is an outstanding choice for any occasion, from business lunches to dinner parties to pre-theater cocktails.

PORK MEDALLIONS
With Huckleberry Sauce

WILD RICE
1 cup wild rice
2 cups water
1/2 medium red bell pepper, finely diced
2 Tbsp. butter
1 Tbsp. chopped parsley
Salt and pepper to taste

1. Simmer the rice in water, covered for 30–40 minutes until tender. Meanwhile, saute the red bell pepper in the butter until just tender. Remove from heat and add chopped parsley. When rice is tender, stir in the butter and red pepper mixture. Season with salt and pepper to taste. Cover and keep in a warm place until ready to serve.

PORK MEDALLIONS AND SAUCE
4 6–8 oz. boneless, trimmed pork loin (center–cut medallions)
1 1/2 cups reduced veal or chicken stock
1/2 cup fresh or frozen huckleberries or blueberries (The huckleberries are worth trying to find!)
3 Tbsp. cold, unsalted butter
1 Tbsp. snipped chives
Salt and pepper to taste

1. Place the pork medallions between two sheets of waxed paper and with a meat tenderizer or rolling pin, firmly pound the pork into medallions 1" to 1 1/2" thick. Season with salt and pepper.

2. In a large, heavy saute pan, saute medallions in 1 Tbsp. of the butter until desired doneness (approximately 5–7 minutes per side). If necessary, lower heat so medallions don't brown. Keep medallions warm while finishing the sauce.

3. With the same saute pan, pour off any excess fat and return to stove. Over high heat, pour in the chicken or veal stock, stirring and scraping the pork residue from the bottom of the pan. Reduce the mixture to 1/2 cup (approximately 5 minutes), then stir into the berries and remaining 2 Tbsp. of butter. Check the seasoning.

4. When the butter is incorporated, the sauce should be slightly thickened and rich tasting.

5. Pour the warm wild rice in the center of a large serving platter and arrange the medallions over the rice. Spoon sauce over and around the pork medallions. Sprinkle with the snipped chives and serve immediately.

SERVES 4

TRI CHOCOLATE MOUSSE CAKE

**FIRST LAYER –
DARK CHOCOLATE**
2 cups bittersweet chocolate,
  chopped
7 Tbsp. butter
2 tsp. instant coffee
2 tsp. warm water
1/2 tsp. unflavored gelatin
4 eggs, separated
1/4 tsp. cream of tartar
1/4 cup sugar

1. Place chocolate and butter in a stainless bowl over simmering water, not boiling. Stir with a spatula until melted and smooth. Dissolve the gelatin and coffee in the warm water and add to the melted chocolate, stirring all the while.

2. Beat the egg yolks and add to the mixture. Beat the whites until soft peaked and add the cream of tartar, continuing to beat. Add the sugar and beat until firm peaks will hold. Fold the chocolate mixture into the whites only until mixed.

3. Turn into an 8" removable bottom cheesecake pan that has a parchment lined bottom. Smooth the layer and clean the sides of the pan. Refrigerate until second layer is prepared.

**SECOND LAYER –
MILK CHOCOLATE**
2 cups milk chocolate, chopped
2 tsp. instant coffee
1/4 cup warm water
1/2 tsp. unflavored gelatin
1 1/4 cups heavy cream

4. Soften gelatin in the warm water and add the instant coffee. Place over simmering water and stir until smooth and completely melted. Add the chopped chocolate and stir over warm water, not boiling, until chocolate is smooth. Do not let the chocolate get hot, only melted. Remove from heat and stir to cool somewhat. Whip the cream until firm and fold the chocolate into it. Turn into the pan on top of the dark chocolate layer and smooth. Chill until the top layer is complete.

**THIRD LAYER –
WHITE CHOCOLATE**
2 cups white chocolate, chopped
1/2 tsp. gelatin
1/4 cup warm water
1 1/3 cups heavy cream

5. Soften gelatin in water and heat until just melted. Add chopped chocolate and remove from heat. Stir until chocolate is melted and smooth. Whip the cream until firm and fold the chocolate mixture into it. Turn into the mold and smooth the top. Let mousse chill overnight, unmold and serve. Decorate with chocolate shavings or chocolate cut-outs.

63

SERVES 10–12

PARK CAFE

A walk in the park will take you to a place with a light, airy atmosphere and nouveau cuisine. Located next to Liberty Park, the Park Cafe offers a wonderful array of fresh dishes throughout the day. Stroll through the wide selection of breakfast pastries, luncheon salads and sandwiches, or distinctive dinner entrees.

The cafe atmosphere is relaxed and is great for lunch with friends or convenient for a business lunch. Weather allowing, they also have a charming deck for nourishment outdoors.

So wander over to the Park Cafe, and don't forget the most enjoyable tour of all – the extensive assortment of celebrated desserts!

PINE NUT TART

1/2 stick butter
1/4 lb. almond paste
1 cup sugar
8 eggs
1 cup light corn syrup
1/4 tsp. salt
1/4 tsp. vanilla

1. Cream together butter and almond paste.

2. Add sugar, then eggs and corn syrup, salt and vanilla.

3. In a 12" tart pan, line a partially baked tart shell with pine nuts, fill with above mixture and bake at 350 degrees until golden brown for about 20 minutes.

SERVES 8–10

FYI:

~ *Almonds can be used instead of pine nuts if a substitute is needed.*

~ *We recommend that you use a sweet tart shell crust recipe.*

STICK BUNS

2 sticks butter
1 cup brown sugar
1/2 Tbsp. salt
4 eggs
2 cups pumpkin
2 Tbsp. yeast
3 cups warm water
12 cups flour

1. Cream together butter, sugar and salt. Add eggs, then pumpkin.

2. Combine warm water with yeast to activate.

3. Add flour and yeast mixture to ingredients and knead until elastic. Let rise once, punch down and let rise again.

6 sticks butter
3 cups brown sugar

4. Beat together until creamy.

5. Roll dough into rectangle and spread with the butter and sugar mixture.

6. Sprinkle with nuts and cinnamon, roll up jelly-roll fashion. Cut into 1 inch lengths, lay out on sheet pan and let rise until doubled. Bake at 350 degrees 18–20 minutes.

SERVES 12

FYI:

- Take care not to overcook!

SALT LAKE ROASTING COMPANY

"Life is too short to drink bad coffee."

And many Salt Lake residents heartily agree. With the most dedicated, yet varied clientele, the Salt Lake Roasting Company consistently provides "coffee without compromise."

The wide selection of delectible pastries and desserts are too tempting to skip. And the daily surprises in savory lunch and dinner items offer mouth-watering alternatives, cafe style.

If you're not willing to compromise when it comes to good coffee, make sure it's from the Salt Lake Roasting Company.

Because life is too short!

CAFE MOCHA

Good, strong coffee
8 or 10 oz. tall glass mugs
Dutch Cocoa
   (24% cocoa butter content)
Hot milk (2 oz. per serving)

1. Begin with good, strong coffee, prepared as described below.

2. Fill the mugs 3/4 full with coffee.

3. Stir in a heaping spoonful of cocoa.

4. Top off glass with steamed milk.

5. Sweeten as desired.

6. Sprinkle with powdered cocoa.

FYI: (How to Make Good Coffee at Home)

~ *Excellent coffee begins with water that is cool, fresh and clear.*

~ *Always use high quality coffee that has been recently roasted.*

~ *Grind coffee just before brewing, making sure the grind corresponds to the method of brewing (coarse for press pot, very fine for espresso).*

~ *Bring water just to boiling, 195 to 205 degrees.*

~ *Make sure your brewing equipment is clean.*

~ *Measure coffee and water accurately, do not guess: Strong coffee = 2 tablespoons per 1 cup of water.*

~ *Serve immediately. Good coffee is unbeatable but never reheatable!!*

QUICHE

One pie shell
4 eggs
1 cup milk
1 cup cream
Salt to taste
Pepper to taste
Nutmeg to taste
1 cup filling (approximate)

1. Whip eggs, milk, cream and seasonings in a metal bowl with a wire whip just until mixed.

2. Place filling of choice in bottom of pie shell.

3. Pour ingredients in bowl into pie shell.

4. Bake in oven at 375 degrees until golden brown and puffy (about 30 minutes).

CHICKEN FILLING
1/2 cup cooked, diced chicken
1/4 cup diced bell pepper
1/2 cup fontina or gouda cheese

SERVES 4

SHRIMP FILLING
1/2 cup shrimp (raw or cooked)
1 clove chopped garlic
1 chopped avocado
1/3 cup crumbled brie

VEGETABLE FILLING
1 cup chopped veggies
1/2 cup grated cheddar cheese
1 Tbsp. chopped, fresh basil

FYI:

~ If only milk is used, the quiche will be a lighter, custard style. If all cream is used, it will be quite rich.

SHALLOW SHAFT

The spirit of adventure brought silver mining to
Alta in the 1800's. Nowadays, descendants of
those early miners can be found roaming the
mountainsides on skis, bikes, and boots.

The Shallow Shaft Restaurant is a favorite gathering
spot for Alta's modern day adventurers. The rustic
atmosphere of the Shallow Shaft complements the
rugged beauty of its surroundings.

The Chef has drawn from influences of the
American Southwest, Pacific Northwest, and a
hint of France to create a menu that reflects the
tastes of today's discriminating thrill-seeker.
Come in and discover the marinated chicken with
kiwi salsa, exotic pizzas, or Steak Neptune, all
enhanced by crisp, mountain air. All they
ask is that you leave your pick at the door.

GRILLED CHICKEN
With Kiwi Salsa

6 large (8 oz.) boneless,
skinless chicken breasts

MARINADE
1/2 cup olive oil
1/2 cup dry vermouth
4 large shallots
4 large garlic cloves
1/2 cup fresh cilantro
1 Tbsp. ground cumin
1 tsp. chili powder
1 tsp. salt

1. Peel the garlic and shallots. In a food processor, combine the olive oil, vermouth, shallots, garlic, cilantro, cumin, chili powder and salt. Puree until smooth (about 2 minutes).

2. Place the marinade into a non–reactive container such as glass or stainless steel. Add the chicken breasts. Make sure that the chicken is completely covered with the marinade. Cover and set aside for at least one hour.

SALSA
3 large kiwis
3 very red roma tomatoes
Cilantro
Olive oil
Balsamic vinegar
Salt

3. Peel the kiwis. Core or otherwise de–seed the tomatoes. Chop both into 1/2" dices.

4. Add a splash of olive oil and balsamic vinegar. Add chopped cilantro and salt to taste.

5. On a barbecue or under a broiler, cook the chicken until it is firm to the touch (about 6–8 minutes). Garnish with salsa.

SERVES 6

FYI:

~ This unbelievable chicken dish is an excellent choice for casual entertaining! We strongly recommend cooking the chicken on the barbecue.

~ The salsa recipe is flexible. Vary it by adding ingredients such as jicama.

BEAR LAKE RASPBERRIES
With Framboise Créme Fraîche

6 cups fresh Bear Lake
  raspberries
1 quart whipping cream
1 cup sour cream
1/2 cup powdered sugar
1/2 cup Framboise liqueur

1. Put the cream, sugar, and sour cream into a stainless mixing bowl. Mix well. Let the cream mixture sit out at room temperature overnight or until it reaches the consistency of homemade yogurt.

2. After it has thickened, mix in the Framboise liqueur and refrigerate.

3. To serve, put about half of the berries in a serving bowl, top with the créme fraîche, then top with the rest of the berries. For a particularly attractive dessert, add another layer made from whipped cream, flavored with peppermint schnapps. Garnish with mint leaves and a few more of the biggest and ripest berries.

SERVES 6

FYI:

~ This dessert features one of the most delectable berries available anywhere, the Bear Lake raspberry. A suggested addition ~ serve with some fresh sugar cookies.

SQUATTER'S PUB BREWERY

It's Friday afternoon and it's been a long week. Your mind wanders towards the weekend and you know you need to start it off right. Socialize this evening in a comfortable atmosphere with good friends, good spirits, and good food – head to Squatter's Pub Brewery. It's the best beer you'll find in Salt Lake, with the widest varieties in taste and styles – all made on the premises.

The outside patio is a relaxing delight in good weather. The pleasant atmosphere complements the food which includes a wide array of upscale pub cuisine – everything from Fish 'n' Chips to Pesto Pizza, delectable pasta specials, and spicy Buffalo Wings.

It's a great place for having lunch, meeting friends after work, and enjoying one of Salt Lake's finest casual eating establishments.

Is it five o'clock yet?

PESTO PIZZA

1/2 lb. basil
1 bunch parsley
1 cup toasted pinenuts
1/4 cup asiago cheese
2 Tbsp. garlic puree
Salt and pepper to taste

1. Process these ingredients. Texture should be almost a puree.

1/8 cup finely chopped rosemary
1/4 cup chopped yellow onions

2. Saute the onions and rosemary until onions are soft. Set aside.

4 cups high gluten flour
1 Tbsp. salt
1/4 cup olive oil
3/4 oz. yeast
1/8 cup sugar
1 1/2 cup warm water

3. In a mixing bowl combine the flour, salt, olive oil and onion mixture and set aside.

4. In a separate bowl, combine the water and sugar and stir until sugar is dissolved. Stir in the yeast and let stand for 5 minutes until yeast activates.

5. Combine with flour mixture and cover with a towel. Let rise for 30 minutes, portion it, and let it rise overnight.

6. Roll dough out and spread the pesto on first, then tomato slices and top with mozzarella cheese and whatever else you would like.

7. Bake at 475 degrees for approximately 8–10 minutes or until crust is brown and cheese is browned.

SERVES 6

FYI:

~ *You can substitue all-purpose flour for the high gluten flour if desired.*

PLUM WALNUT BBQ SAUCE

1 cup hoisin sauce
1 cup plum sauce
1 cup soy sauce
1/2 cup molasses
1 Tbsp. garlic puree
2 Tbsp. brown sugar
1 Tbsp. chili powder
1/2 Tbsp. fresh ginger
1 cup finely chopped walnuts

1. Mix all ingredients together in large bowl.

2. Use for grilled chicken or pork.

SERVES 8-10

FYI:

- *You can get the hoisin sauce and plum sauce at Oriental markets or most grocery stores.*

- *The smaller the walnuts are chopped, the better they will stick to the meat.*

S U N D A N C E

Sundance invites you to experience candlelight
dining in the rustic elegance of the Tree Room. The
sumptuous entrees are accented by herbs, spices and edible
flowers which are grown on the premises. Native American art and Western
memorabilia from Robert Redford's personal collection grace this
harmonious setting.

The resort of Sundance offers the beauty of the Tree Room
as well as the informal atmosphere of The Grill Room, located
next door. The Grill Room features lighter, bistro style fare and is
an ideal place for an appetizing lunch or casual dinner.

The many delightful outdoor activities at Sundance also provide residents and
visitors with year-round enjoyment in a splendid and refreshing setting.

PECAN CRUSTED
CHICKEN
With Apple Cider Sauce

6 boneless, skinless
  chicken breasts
1 cup flour
2 eggs
1 cup milk
1 cup finely chopped pecans
1/4 cup bread crumbs

1. Combine pecans and breadcrumbs.

2. Mix eggs and milk.

3. Place chicken in flour, then milk and eggs, and finish in pecans.

4. Heat a skillet with oil and pan fry until brown.

5. Bake in 350 degree oven until done.

APPLE CIDER SAUCE
1 Tbsp. olive oil
3 shallots
1 Tbsp. minced garlic
1 quart cider
2 cups demi-glace
1/2 cup heavy cream
Salt and pepper to taste

6. Place oil in sauce pan and heat. Saute shallots and garlic.

7. Add cider and simmer until reduced by half.

8. Add remaining ingredients and simmer until thick.

SERVES 6

FYI:

- Knorr's Demi-Glace in a dry package mix can be used for this amazing sauce.

COCONUT SHRIMP
With Mango Lime Sauce

SHRIMP
2 lbs. shrimp, peeled and
  deveined
1 lb. shredded coconut
3 cups flour
4 eggs
1 can beer
2 Tbsp. cajun spice

1. Combine 1 1/2 cups flour, eggs, beer and cajun spice. Mix well.

2. Place shrimp in remaining flour, then place in batter and finish in coconut.

3. Deep fry shrimp in 325 degree vegetable oil until brown.

MANGO LIME SAUCE
2 cups pureed mangos
2 tsp. pureed ginger
2 Tbsp. lime juice
2 Tbsp. honey
2 Tbsp. rice vinegar

4. Combine all ingredients and mix well.

SERVES 8

FYI:

~ *This appetizer is one of our absolute favorites! Either medium or large size shrimp can be used for this recipe.*

~ *Make sure to use cajun spice and not cajun seasoning, which is a seasoned salt.*

TOUCAN CANTINA
BAJA CANTINA

One isn't enough when it comes to unbeatable Mexican food. So there are two popular locations for locals or visitors who need to satisfy a Mexican craving.

Baja Cantina (in Park City) and Toucan Cantina (in Salt Lake) offer exceptional menus in a lively atmosphere, guaranteed to enhance your spirits and your appetite. Fresh salsa, great margaritas, and hearty entrees make either location a good bet when you're in the mood for Mexican.

After a day on the slopes or in the shops, drop into Baja Cantina and unwind with traditional Mexican food in comfortable surroundings. The big screen TV and bar at Toucan Cantina make it fun for game days, holidays, or a night out with friends. Ole!

TJ TAXI

1 1/2 lb. boneless, skinless
  chicken breasts
6 eight inch flour tortillas
1 cup sour cream
1 cup diced onion
1 1/2 cup fresh diced tomatoes
4 cups shredded cheddar cheese
Salt and pepper to taste

1. Slice chicken into 1/2 inch strips.

2. Season chicken and cook over medium to high heat using 1 Tbsp. oil until brown.

3. Lay tortillas flat. Spread equal amount of sour cream on tortillas. Add diced onion, diced tomatoes, 1 1/2 cup cheese, and chicken.

4. Roll, and top with remainder of cheese.

5. Bake for 15–20 minutes at 350 degrees or or until cheese is melted. Top with guacamole and serve immediately.

SERVES 6

FYI:

~ If you want a spicy version, season your chicken with cilantro, cumin, chili powder, or your favorite Mexican spices.

MULEGE BANANA

6 ripe bananas
1/4 stick butter
1/4 cup brown sugar
1/8 cup brandy
Cinnamon to taste
Nutmeg to taste

1. Peel and cut bananas in half, length-wise.

2. Mix melted butter, brown sugar, and brandy.

3. Pour mixture over bananas. Dust with cinnamon, and microwave 30 seconds.

4. Bake in oven 4–5 minutes in 350 degree oven.

5. Top with 1 scoop vanilla ice cream and nutmeg.

SERVES 6

FYI:

- *This simple recipe makes an easy, but unique dessert!*

W . H . BRUMBY'S

Gourmet food has never been this easy.

A quick stop into W.H. Brumby's will offer you a wide assortment of superb
specials at any time of the day. Breakfast and savory pastries, green or pasta
salads, homemade soups, breads, fresh locally-roasted coffee, sandwiches,
and elegant desserts are presented daily.

Located near the University of Utah, W.H. Brumby's is a favorite for students,
academics, and business professionals. W.H. Brumby's is frequented by deli,
bakery, and coffee connoisseurs whose
pursuit of quality is satisfied with the
stylish presentation found here.

And if you'd like an evening of
entertaining without spending
the day in the kitchen, dash
into Brumby's for impressive
dishes your guests are sure
to remember!

SPANISH GAZPACHO

2 lbs. fresh tomatoes, peeled
    and diced finely
1 lb. canned Italian tomatoes,
    diced finely
1 red onion, diced finely
1 red pepper, diced finely
1 green pepper, diced finely
1 cucumber, seeded and
    diced finely
1 thick slice stale bread,
    crust removed
1 whole egg
2 cloves fresh garlic
1/4 cup best Italian olive oil
1 Tbsp. balsamic vinegar
1 Tbps. tomato paste
Salt to taste
Fresh ground pepper to taste

1. Prepare vegetables as directed, set aside half of each.

2. In a food processor, put the bread, garlic and egg. Slowly add the oil. Should be the consistency of a thick paste.

3. Add the vinegar and tomato paste. Next, add half the prepared vegetables. Process until liquidized.

4. Remove from processor, add the reserved vegetables.

5. Chill thoroughly before serving.

6. Add tomato juice or V8 if a thinner soup is required.

SERVES 6-8

FYI:

- *This wonderful soup can be served with crushed ice and a side of good, crusty bread.*

FRESH FRUIT TART

SUGAR CRUST
6 Tbsp. butter (room temp)
2 Tbsp. sugar
1/4 tsp. vanilla sugar
Pinch of salt
1 scant cup flour
1/2 a beaten egg

1. In a mixing bowl, blend together butter, sugar, vanilla sugar, and flour. Then add the egg. Mix rapidly. Do not overwork. Wrap well in plastic wrap and store in refrigerator for a minimum of 1 hour.

2. Roll the dough on a lightly floured table to about 1/8". Line a 9" tart pan or flan ring with dough. Cut excess dough with a knife or by rolling the rolling pin over the top.

3. Prick bottom of shell with fork and then line shell with parchment paper and fill with lentils or beans to prevent shell from bubbling. Bake for 15–25 minutes at 350 degrees. Remove from oven and allow to cool.

CUSTARD
1 cup milk
1/4 vanilla bean, split in half
    lengthwise
3 egg yolks
1/3 cup granulated sugar
2 Tbsp. cornstarch or flour

1. Heat milk and vanilla bean to a simmer. Whisk sugar and egg yolks until ribbon consistency. Gently pour in the cornstarch or flour with a whisk. Pour hot milk through strainer into the egg mixture, beating all the time.

2. Pour this mixture back into the sauce pan and bring to a slow boil again, whisking constantly so the mixture doesn't stick to the pan. Allow to boil for one minute, stirring vigorously. Pour into bowl and cover with plastic wrap to prevent skin from forming. Allow to cool.

FRUIT AND GLAZE
Strawberries
Kiwi
Raspberries
Blackberries
And other seasonal fruit
2 Tbsp. apricot preserves

1. Fill pastry shell with custard. Arrange the fruit evenly on top of the custard so that the whole tart is covered.

2. Heat apricot preserve in a pan until melted. Strain through a seive. Using a pastry brush, brush the fruit thickly with the apricot glaze.

SERVES 6–8

American Grill (Cottonwood)
4835 S. Highland Drive
Holladay, Utah
801-277-7082

Baja Cantina
1284 Empire Avenue
Park City, Utah
801-649-2252

American Grill (Downtown)
280 S. Main
SLC, Utah
801-363-6935

The Bistro Royale
1500 Kearns Blvd.
Park City, Utah
801-649-1799

Archibald's
1095 W. 7800 S.
West Jordan, Utah
801-566-6940

Cafe Pierpont
122 W. Pierpont Ave.
SLC, Utah
801-364-1222

Cafe Terigo
424 Main Street
Park City, Utah
801-645-9555

Charlie Chow
Trolley Square
SLC, Utah
801-575-6700

E.I.B.O.S.
Famous For Nothing
Mesquite Broiler

E.I.B.O.'S Famous for Nothing
300 Trolley Square
SLC, Utah
801-531-7788

Ferrantelli
300 Trolley Square
SLC, Utah
801-531-8228

Cisero's
306 Main Street
Park City, Utah
801-649-5044

Giovanni's
11491 Big Cottonwood Canyon
Brighton, Utah
801-364-4484

Hibachi
238 E. South Temple
SLC, Utah
801-364-5456

Lamb's
169 S. Main
SLC, Utah
801-364-7166

Hungry I
1440 S. Foothill Drive
SLC, Utah
801-582-8600

Mandarin Restaurant
348 E. 900 N.
Bountiful, Utah
801-298-2406

La Caille at Quail Run
9565 Wasatch Blvd.
Sandy, Utah
801-942-1751

Market Street Broiler
260 S. 1300 E.
SLC, Utah
801-583-8808

McHenry's Grill
Deer Valley Resort
Silverlake Lodge
Park City, Utah
801-649-1000

Millcreek Inn
Millcreek Canyon
Holladay, Utah
801-278-7927

Mikado
67 W. 100 S.
SLC, Utah
801-328-0929

The New Yorker
60 W. Market Street
SLC, Utah
801-363-0166

Mileti's
412 Main Street
Park City, Utah
801-649-8211

Park Cafe
604 E. 1300 S.
SLC, Utah
801-487-1670

the Salt Lake Roasting Co.

SUNDANCE

Salt Lake Roasting Co.
320 E. 400 S.
SLC, Utah
801-363-7572

Sundance
North Fork Provo Canyon
Sundance, Utah
801-225-4107

The Shallow Shaft Restaurant
P.O. Box 8029
Alta, Utah
801-742-2177

Toucan Cantina
4800 S. 1790 E.
SLC, Utah
801-272-1044

Squatter's Pub Brewery
147 W. 300 S.
SLC, Utah
801-363-2739

W. H. Brumby's
224 S. 1300 E.
SLC, Utah
801-581-0888

APPETIZERS

Coconut Shrimp with Mango Lime Sauce   78

Crab Cakes   48

Pot Stickers   18

Salmon Rolls   38

Stuffed Mushrooms   20

Sun-Dried Tomato and Pesto Mascarpone Terrine   50

Texas BBQ Shrimp   57

SOUPS

Avgolemeno Soup   35

Gorgonzola Mushroom Soup   30

Minestrone Soup   26

Spanish Gazpacho   83

Spring Pea Soup   14

Tortilla Soup   3

SALADS

Japanese Salad   33

Pollo Salad   11

Spinach Salad with Hot Bacon Dressing   5

Wonton Salad   24

ENTREES

Barbecued Lamb Shanks   41

Beef and Asparagus with Black Bean Sauce   44

Beef Sukiyaki   54

Black Tiger Prawns, Thai Style   39

Chicken Lorraine   60

Chicken Teriyaki   32

Chicken Tostada   12

Crab Cakes   48

Grilled Chicken with Kiwi Salsa   71

Halibut Casserole with Tater Chips   6

Firecracker Noodles with Char Sui Pork   17

Marinated Veal Chops   27

Millcreek Duck   59

Mountain Trout   53

Pecan Crusted Chicken with Apple Cider Sauce   77

Pepper Steak   29

Pesto Lasagna   56

Pesto Pizza   74

Phoenix and Dragon   45

ENTREES (Continued)

Pork Medallions with Huckleberry Sauce   62

Psari Plaki   36

Quiche   69

Salmon Dill Fettuccini   15

Salmon Scallopini   8

Spinach Fettuccini with Chicken, Prosciutto, and Mushrooms   2

TJ Taxi   80

Veal Piccata   21

SAUCES

Apple Cider Sauce   77

Kiwi Salsa   71

Mango Lime Sauce   78

Plum Walnut BBQ Sauce   75

Tartar Sauce   48

Watermelon BBQ Sauce   23